100 EASY CLASSICS is a collection of well-known tunes from the world of song, folk music, opera, 'the classics', ballet and light music. The pieces — over 40 composers are represented in the book — vary in style from the swaying ***Barcarolle*** of Offenbach's ***Tales of Hoffmann*** to the strident ***La Donna e Mobile*** from Verdi's ***Rigoletto***; from the delicacy of the ***Pizzicato Polka*** to the rhythmical vitality of Chabrier's Spanish rhapsody, ***Espana***.

The pieces have been arranged with the inexperienced player particularly in mind; the melody, for instance, often appears as single notes only, with the left hand supplying a straightforward accompaniment; many of the tunes (such as the *Minute Waltz* by Chopin) have been transposed into simpler keys from their counterparts of more sharps or flats, and occasionally some of the original decorative piano figuration has been simplified.

The result is a veritable treasury of all-time best-loved music arranged for piano.

First Published 1985

138 Charing Cross Road, London WC2H 0LD

Exclusive Distributors
International Music Publications
Southend Road, Woodford Green,
Essex IG8 8HN, England.

AIR (from *The Water Music*)

Handel

f
dim.
p
mf
p
mf
dim.
pp

AIR ON A G STRING

Bach

poco cresc.
f
dim.
p
cresc.
mf
3
dim. e rall.

ARTIST'S LIFE

Strauss

pp
f
Fine
p
f
D.C. al Fine

AVE MARIA

Schubert

p
sempre p
dim. e rit.
pp

BALLET MUSIC (from *Rosamunde*)

Schubert

Andantino
f
Andante
pp
mf
f
D.C. al Fine.

BARCAROLLE (from *The Tales of Hoffmann*)

Offenbach

cresc.
f
rall.
p a tempo
cresc. molto
ff
p
p rall.

BLACK EYES

Russian Gipsy Song

decresc.
Fine
f
f
D.𝄋 al Fine

BLUE DANUBE WALTZ

Strauss

p
f
p
f
mf
p
p
D.C. al Fine.

BRIDAL MARCH (from *Lohengrin*)

Wagner

f
cresc.
ff
p
pp
Ped.

THE CELEBRATED GALOP

(from *Orpheus in the Underworld*)

Offenbach

mp
mf

CHANSON TRISTE

Tschaikovsky

p
cresc.
f
f
poco rit.
D.C.
Coda
pp
rall.

CHANT SANS PAROLES

Tschaikovsky

cresc.
mf
dim.
poco rit.
p a tempo
mf
dim. e rit.

CRADLE SONG (Wiegenlied)

Mozart

poco rit.
p a tempo
rall.

CRADLE SONG

Schubert

mf
pp
p
8va
pp
poco rit.

DANCE OF THE HOURS

Ponchielli

p
sempre p
rit.
p a tempo
cresc.
mf
dim.
poco rit.
p a tempo
cresc.
f
mf
dim. e rit.
p
ff

DANCE OF THE SUGAR PLUM FAIRY

(from *Casse Noisette*)

Tschaikovsky

p

DIE FLEDERMAUS (*The Bat*)

Strauss

p
D.C. al Fine

ESPAÑA

Chabrier

p
mf
p
ff

FANTASIE IMPROMPTU (*Second Movement*)

Cantabile

mp

f
mp
rall.

FLOWER SONG (from *Faust*)

Gounod

cresc.
f
mp

FÜR ELISE

Beethoven

HABANERA (from *Carmen*)

Bizet

mf
f marcato
dim e rit.
a tempo f

HARK, HARK THE LARK

Schubert

pp
mf
p
mf
p
f
p
f
p

HEDGE ROSES

Schubert

R.H. 8va
f
poco rit.
p a tempo
loco
p rit.
p a tempo
f
poco rit.

HUMORESKE (Op 101, No 7)

Dvořák

cresc.
rit.
f a tempo
mf
f
mf
p
dim. e rit.

HUNGARIAN DANCE

Brahms

p

HUNGARIAN RHAPSODY No 2

Liszt

Vivace

mf

marcato

INVITATION TO THE WALTZ

Weber

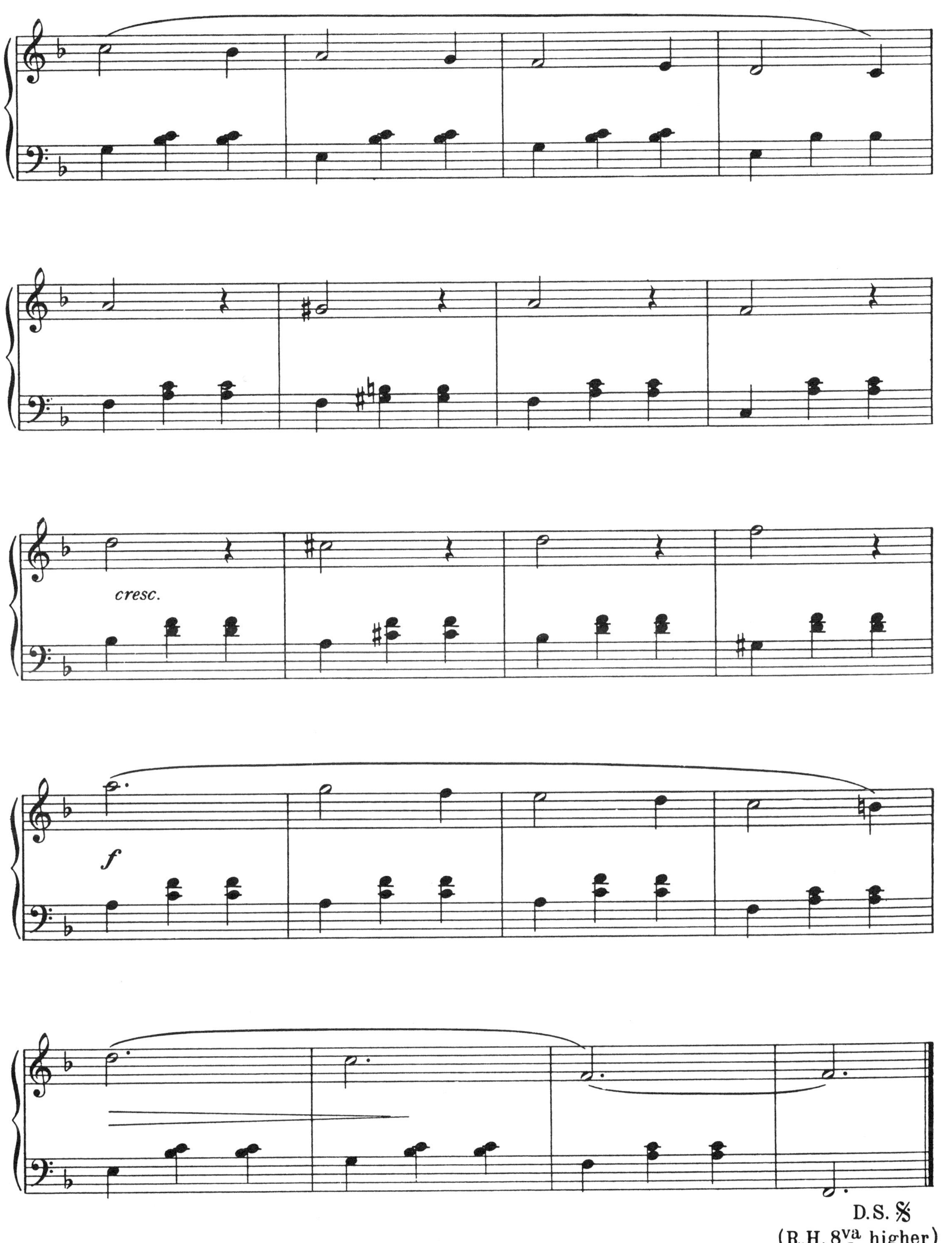
cresc.
f
D.S. 𝄋
(R.H. 8va higher)

LA GOLONDRINA *(The Swallow)*

Serradell

cresc.
f
p
mf
cresc.
f
dim.
mf
cresc.
f
p
dim.
pp

LARGO

Handel

piu f
poco cresc.
sf
dim.
dolce
f
decresc.
rall.
Ped.

LARGO (from the *New World Symphony*)

Dvořák

mf
p
cresc.
p
cresc.
R.H.
L.H.
pp

LIGHT CAVALRY

Suppé

f
f
ff

THE LOST CHORD

Sullivan

p a tempo
cresc.
mf
cresc.
f
Slower
ff
Sempre ff

LOVE'S DREAM

Liszt

Ped.
più smorz e ril.

LULLABY WALTZ

Brahms

poco cresc.

THE MAIDEN'S PRAYER

Badarzewska

p
mf
poco rit.

MARCH (from *Casse Noisette*)

Tschaikovsky

f
p
mf
p
mf p
cresc.
f
p
mf
p
mf p
cresc.
f

MARCH (from *Scipio*)

Handel

f
mf
f
rall.

MARCH (from *Tannhaüser*)

Wagner

Tempo di Marcia

f

mf

f

mf
f

MARCH (from *William Tell*)

Rossini

mf
p
mf
f
ff
ff

MAZURKA (from *Coppélia*)

Delibes

mp

MEDITATION on the Prelude by J S BACH (*Ave Maria*)

Gounod

p
p
p
mf
f
dim.
mf
dim.
mp
rall.
pp

MELODY IN F

Rubinstein

mf
f
dim.
rall.
p
rall.
p
p a tempo
f
rit.

THE MERRY PEASANT

Schumann

cresc.
f
mf
cresc.
f
rall.

THE MERRY WIVES OF WINDSOR

Nicolai

p
mf
f

MILITARY MARCH

Schubert

TRIO
mf
p
p
p
D. C. al Fine.

MINUET IN G

Beethoven

1
2
D.C. al Fine.

MINUTE WALTZ (Op 64, No 1)

Chopin

D.C. al Fine

MOMENT MUSICAL

Schubert

mf
p
pp
poco rit.

MOONLIGHT SONATA

Beethoven

cresc.
dim.
mf
p
dim.
p
pp

MORGENBLÄTTER (*Morning Papers*)

Strauss

D.C. al Fine

MORNING (from *Peer Gynt*)

Grieg

p
cresc.
f
decresc.
p
p
pp

MORNING, NOON AND NIGHT

Suppé

dim.
poco rit.
p a tempo
mf
cresc.
f
ff

NARCISSUS

Nevin

decresc.
Fine
più f
cresc.
ff rall.
D.C. al Fine

NOCTURNE IN E flat

Chopin

pp poco rit.
f a tempo
poco rall.
a tempo
pp

O FOR THE WINGS OF A DOVE

Mendelssohn

f
mf
p
p
pp

ON WINGS OF SONG

Mendelssohn

decresc.
mf
f
mp
allarg.
rall. e decresc.

OVER THE WAVES

Rosas

D. C. al Fine

PAS DES FLEURS (Intermezzo from *Naila*)

Delibes

D.C. al Fine

PIZZICATO (from *Sylvia*)

Delibes

Moderato

p sempre staccato

Fine
Meno mosso
p
D. C. al Fine

PIZZICATO POLKA

Strauss

decresc.
pp
pp
Fine
p
staccato
D.C. al Fine

POET AND PEASANT

Suppé

Tempo di Valse

POLONAISE IN A

Chopin

f
poco rit.
f a tempo
f

POLONAISE IN A FLAT (Op 53)

Chopin

POST HORN GALOP

Koenig

mf
f
D.C. al Fine

RADETZKY MARCH

Strauss

cresc.
f
dim.
p
f

RIGOLETTO (*La Donna è Mobile*)

Verdi

Allegretto

ROMEO AND JULIET WALTZ

Gounod

Fine
D.C.

ROSES FROM THE SOUTH

Strauss

p

SERENADE

Schubert

pp
Ped.
p
f
mf
dim.

SHEEP MAY SAFELY GRAZE

Bach

pp
mf
p
mf
p
pp rit.

THE SKATERS' WALTZ

Waldteufel

cresc.
f
p delicately
mf
ff

THE SLEEPING BEAUTY WALTZ

Tschaikovsky

mf
f
f

SLUMBER SONG (*Schlummerlied*)

Schumann

Fine
mf
D.C. al Fine

SOLDIERS' CHORUS (from *Faust*)

Gounod

p
3
D.C. al Fine

SONATA IN C (K.545)

Mozart

mf
8
8
loco
cresc.
f
dim.
p
mf
p
f
ff

SONATA PATHÉTIQUE

Beethoven

p
p
pp
mp
mf
3
mp
p
pp

SONG OF THE TOREADOR (from *Carmen*)

Bizet

Tempo I
f
mf
simile
f
simile
rall.
ff

SONG OF THE VOLGA BOATMEN

Traditional

mf
rall.
morendo
8va basso

SPRING SONG

Mendelssohn

ten.
f
p
dolce.
mf
rall.
p a tempo
simile
p
cresc.
p con grazia
p
leggiero
p
Ped.

SWAN LAKE WALTZ

Tschaikovsky

f
cresc. poco a poco
ff

TALES FROM THE VIENNA WOODS

Strauss

TANGO

Albeniz

p a tempo
mf
rall.

THEME (from *Concerto in B Flat Minor*)

Tschaikovsky

rall.

THEME (from *Unfinished Symphony*)

Schubert

mp
poco rit.
mf
a tempo
p
poco cresc.
dim.
R.H. 8va
mf
p
poco cresc.
dim.
p
loco

TO A WILD ROSE

MacDowell

f

dim. e rall.

p a tempo

mf

dim.

mp

dim.

p

pp

ppp

TRITSCH-TRATSCH POLKA

Strauss

f
p
cresc.
mf
cresc.
p
p
f

TRUMPET VOLUNTARY

Purcell

mf
f
Slower
ff

VALSE (Op 64, No 2)

Chopin

p
Fine
8
D. C.

VALSE BALLET (from *Coppélia*)

Delibes

Tempo di Valse lente

mp *p* *espress.*

Ped.

cresc.

dim.

Ped.

Più animato
f
p
f
p
rall.
espress.
Ped.
cresc.
dim.
Ped.

VALSE DES FLEURS

Tschaikovsky

f
p
f
p
mf
Fine
mp
più f
decresc.
D.C. al Fine

VOICES OF SPRING

Strauss

p
p
Fine
mp
D C

WALTZ (from *Faust*)

Gounod

mf
cresc.
f
Fine
p con espress.
cresc.
mp
cresc.
p con espress.
cresc.
mp
cresc.
f
D.C. al Fine

WAVES OF THE DANUBE

Ivanovici

D. C. al Fine

WEDDING MARCH

Mendelssohn

WHERE E'ER YOU WALK

Handel

cresc.
f
rall.
mf a tempo
f
dim.
p
cresc.
f
rall.

WHO IS SYLVIA?

Schubert

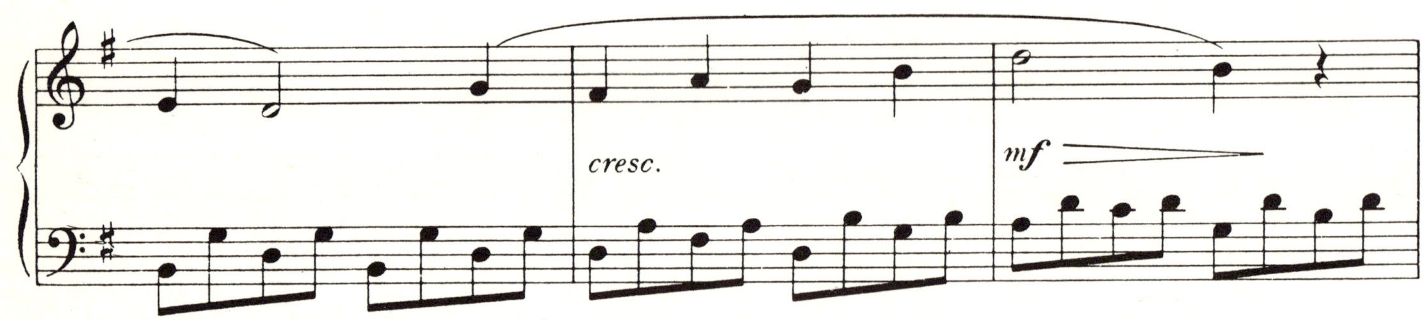

mf
p
mf
f
rall.
p a tempo
rall.

WIENER BLUT

Strauss

p
D.C. al Fine

WINE, WOMAN AND SONG

Strauss

Fine
D.C. al Fine

ZAMPA

Herold

Printed in Great Britain by Hobbs the Printers of Southampton 5/89